EXERCISE BOOKLET
Harold Nelson

The Simon & Schuster
QUICK ACCESS REFERENCE FOR WRITERS

Lynn Quitman Troyka

PRENTICE HALL, *Englewood Cliffs, New Jersey 07632*

©1995 by PRENTICE-HALL, INC.
A Simon and Schuster Company
Englewood Cliffs, New Jersey 07632

10 9 8 7 6 5 4 3 2

ISBN 0-13-127747-2
Printed in the United States of America

A Preface for Instructors

Lynn Quitman Troyka wants writers who use the *Simon & Schuster Quick Access Reference for Writers* "to find whatever information [they] need fast and easily." To help writers do so, she has simplified and shortened *Quick Access* by omitting all exercises.

But many of us who use *Quick Access* in our classes will probably need exercises for quizzes, tests, homework, individualized instruction, supplementary material in a writing lab, questions for contests during class sessions, transparencies on which we demonstrate how to solve specific problems, or as training material for peer tutors. Having the exercises already written will save us preparation time.

This booklet meets this need. It contains sets of supplementary exercises for six sections of *Quick Access*: "Sentence and Word Options," "Correct Grammar," "Punctuation," "Mechanics," and "ESL Information."

Each set contains fifteen exercises. The first five exercises in each set are lettered, and the next ten are numbered. The answer key at the back of this booklet contains answers for the lettered exercises, so students will be able to easily check their own progress. The separate *Answer Key*, which is available to you, contains answers for all of the exercises.

Students are able to buy *Exercise Booklet* at minimal expense. Or, if you prefer, please reprint, photocopy, or make transparencies from the book for use in classes in which you use *Quick Access* as a text.

Harold Nelson
Minot State University
Minot, ND
January, 1995

A Preface for Students

In her "Preface" to *Simon & Schuster Quick Access Reference for Writers*, Lynn Quitman Troyka writes about the power and freedom that knowledge gives each of us. "Students are empowered by knowledge, for it frees us all to enjoy the pleasures of language and to fulfill, with energy and joy, our potential as writers." I agree.

I have kept this idea in mind while writing this *Exercise Booklet*. I want the booklet to help you master the information Ms. Troyka presents in the "Sentence and Word Options," "Correct Grammar," "Punctuation," "Mechanics," and "ESL Information" sections of *QA Ref.* By increasing your knowledge in this way, you will grow in the freedom, power, and joy you feel when you write.

This booklet contains sets of exercises for specific chapters in *QA Ref.* Each set contains five lettered exercises, with answers at the back of this booklet, and ten numbered exercises, with answers in the separate *Answer Key* for instructors. You will learn the most if you review the appropriate chapter immediately before you do a set of exercises, and if you keep in mind the ideas covered in the chapter as you complete the exercises.

When I was a boy, my father would tell me that "practice makes perfect." I have since learned that practice does not necessarily make perfect, but that it does make better. The practice you do in this book should help you grow as a writer.

Harold Nelson
Minot State University
Minot, ND
January, 1995

Contents

Part Two: Sentence and Word Options

Part Three: Correct Grammar

Part Four: Punctuation

Part Five: Mechanics

ESL

7--Conciseness

Revise the following sentences for conciseness if necessary. Example:

The jacket is red, ~~in color.~~
        ∧

a. As a matter of fact, I liked the movie.

b. The ambulance driver made a decision to ignore the red light.

c. There are fifteen different sandwiches listed on the menu.

d. John, who is a good athlete, wants to play professional football.

e. The bill that was introduced into the House was introduced by the speaker.

1. In my opinion, the potato salad needs more salt.

2. As a matter of fact, statistics show that in the case of the generation of baby-boomers, most baby-boomers prefer the incumbent.

3. The incumbent is the type of politician who is honest.

4. Mr. Jones, who is my neighbor, lives in my neighborhood.

5. Your completion of the paper several days before it is due will result in an opportunity for your relaxation immediately before handing in the paper.

6. There are five different meal plans offered by the food service.

7. *The Pale Horse*, which is a detective novel, was written by Agatha Christie.

8. James Butler Hickok was born in 1837 and died in 1876, and he worked as a frontier scout and as a marshal, and he is known as "Wild Bill" Hickok.

9. The authorities contacted the relatives of the passengers who had been injured.

10. The professor's suggestion to Jane is that she increase her motivation if she wants to successfully pass the course.

8--Coordination

Combine the following sentences to illustrate coordination. Do not show coordination in the same way in two successive sentences. Add or delete words or punctuation marks if necessary, but do no major rewriting. Example:

The sky became light. The fog lifted.

a. The French Revolution began in 1789. It ended the thousand-year rule of kings in France.

b. King Louis XVI assembled the French Parliament to deal with France's huge debt. The common people's section of the parliament announced it was France's true legislature.

c. King Louis appeared to disagree with this announcement. A crowd destroyed the royal prison.

d. A constitutional monarchy was established. Some people thought the king would be content.

e. King Louis and the queen, Marie Antoinette, tried to leave the country. They were caught, convicted of treason, and executed on the guillotine.

1. People in the Pacific Northwest call clams *steamers*. People in New England call clams *quahogs*.

2. Littleneck clams are small. They are the tenderest and sweetest type of East Coast hardshells.

3. Surf clams are also West Coast hardshells. They are much larger and tougher than the littlenecks.

4. Littlenecks are normally steamed. Surf clams are normally minced for chowder or cut into strips for frying.

5. The East Coast provides most of the commercial clams produced in the United States. The West Coast provides fewer and less common varieties.

2

6. Strong northern winds blow off Lake Michigan and into Chicago in winter. Chicago is nicknamed the "Windy City."

7. Parents and children often look alike. Children are not duplicates of their parents.

8. Weather forecasters predict a blizzard. They predict high winds and heavy snowfall.

9. The blizzard might come tomorrow. It might come tonight.

10. The shops will close early. The blizzard will come.

8--Subordination

Combine the following sentences to illustrate subordination. Do not show subordination in the same way in two successive sentences. Add or delete words or punctuation marks if necessary, but do no major rewriting. The event recorded in the first sentence occurred before the event recorded in the second. Example:

When +
The sky became light, The fog lifted.

a. The French Revolution began in 1789. It ended the thousand-year rule of kings in France.

b. King Louis XVI assembled the French Parliament to deal with France's huge debt. The common people's section of the parliament announced it was France's true legislature.

c. King Louis appeared to disagree with this announcement. A crowd destroyed the royal prison.

d. A constitutional monarchy was established. Some people thought the king would be content.

e. King Louis and the queen, Marie Antoinette, tried to leave the country. They were caught, convicted of treason, and executed on the guillotine.

1. People in the Pacific Northwest call clams *steamers*. People in New England call clams *quahogs*.

2. Littleneck clams are small. They are the tenderest and sweetest type of East Coast hardshells.

3. Surf clams are also West Coast hardshells. They are much larger and tougher than the littlenecks.

4. Littlenecks are normally steamed. Surf clams are normally minced for chowder or cut into strips for frying.

4

5. The East Coast provides most of the commercial clams produced in the United States. The West Coast provides fewer and less common varieties.

6. Strong northern winds blow off Lake Michigan and into Chicago in winter. Chicago is nicknamed the "Windy City."

7. Parents and children often look alike. Children are not duplicates of their parents.

8. Weather forecasters predict a blizzard. They predict high winds and heavy snowfall.

9. The blizzard might come tomorrow. It might come tonight.

10. The shops will close early. The blizzard will come.

8--Coordination and Subordination

When necessary, clarify coordination or subordination in the following sentences by revising them. Example:

The car was dirty, rusty, and͏ it had been manufactured many years ago.
                          old.

a. The house was large, old, and drafts blew under its doors and windows.

b. After he pleaded no contest to charges of income tax evasion in 1973, Vice President Spiro Agnew resigned his office.

c. The bottom line is the line which shows profit or loss.

d. People often extend this literal meaning of bottom line, and they use the phrase to mean the determining consideration in a decision.

e. Although he confessed his guilt, the bottom line was that Spiro Agnew could no longer serve as vice president.

1. The cat is large, gray and it likes people.

2. The cat, which belongs to my sister, who is older than I am, sleeps at least eighteen hours every day.

3. My sister has a cat, and which I like.

4. My sister has a cat, and I have a dog.

5. My sister likes my dog, and my sister generally likes animals.

6. Cesar Chavez, who founded the National Farm Workers Association in 1962, was born in 1927.

7. Cesar Chavez was a Mexican-American who lived in California, and many of the farm workers he organized into the National Farm Workers Association were also Mexican-Americans, and these farm workers lived in California.

6

8. The National Farm Workers Association led nationwide boycotts against the table grape and the lettuce industries in the 1960s and 1970s, Chavez and the union gained national recognition.

9. Chavez believed in nonviolent resistance, although the National Farm Workers Association used this principle in its boycotts.

10. Chavez was known as an effective speaker and a tireless worker.

9--Parallelism

Revise those sentences which illustrate faulty parallelism. **Example:**

Professor Smith recommends studying the text and ~~to~~ attend⌃class. *(ing)*

a. Archimedes was an ancient Greek scientist, mathematician and he made inventions.

b. According to legend, Archimedes is supposed to have said "Give me the place to stand, and a lever long enough, and I will move the earth," to have shouted "Eureka!" when he stepped into his bath and realized that he could measure the volume of an object by determining the volume of the water it displaces when submerged.

c. Archimedes discovered the principle of buoyancy, he discovered formulas for calculating the area of various geometric figures, and he is remembered as the inventor of the Archimidean screw.

d. According to the principle of buoyancy, a boat floats, or balloons rise because it weighs less than the water or air it displaces.

e. Math students still study the formulas Archimedes discovered in geometry, and engineering students still study his ideas about applying geometry to hydrostatics and mechanics.

1. I've felt tired, grumpy, and with an upset stomach.

2. My doctor recommends that I lose ten pounds, exercise each day, and to sleep at least seven hours each night.

3. I'll follow my doctor's advice because I want to look better and because I want to feel better.

4. Sloppy living can lead not only to physical ailments, but also to a negative attitude.

5. I've joined a health club, I've gone on a diet, and I'm following my doctor's advice.

6. My warm-up includes stretches, pushups, and doing walking.

7. My workouts include playing basketball, climbing stairs, and jumping rope.

8

8. Many people don't exercise enough because they think they don't have time and because of the softness of their couches.

9. Expectations of immediate results from exercise can lead not only to disappointment, but also to anger.

10. I took years to reach this condition, so I expect I will take months to significantly change the condition.

9--Sentence Length

Follow the directions in parentheses after each of the following sentences.
Example:

$$\text{such as \textbar}$$

An acid is a sour-tasting substance$_\wedge$ ~~L~~emon juice$_,$ ~~is an acid. Acid~~ $\overset{which}{\wedge}$ often

dissolves other materials. (Combine into one sentence.)

a. Edward Teller was born in Hungary in 1908, and is an American physicist, and is

   often called the "Father of the Hydrogen Bomb." (Rewrite as two sentences.)

b. The dog barked. (Add an adjective.)

c. The dog barked. (Add an adverb.)

d. The dog barked. (Add an adverb clause.)

e. The dog barked. (Add an adjective clause.)

1. Hemophilia is an inherited disease. It is caused by a deficiency or abnormality of one

   of the clotting factors. These factors are in the blood. Hemophiliacs can bleed to

   death from even small cuts or bruises. (Combine into one sentence.)

2. The dog jumped into the pond. (Invert the word order by placing the verb before the

   subject.)

3. The wind blew. (Add an adjective.)

4. The wind blew. (Add an adverb.)

5. The wind blew. (Add a prepositional phrase.)

6. The wind blew. (Add a participial phrase.)

7. The wind blew. (Add an absolute phrase.)

8. The wind blew. (Add an adverb phrase.)

9. The wind blew. (Add an adverb clause.)

10. The wind blew. (Add an adjective clause.)

10--Word Meanings

© 1995 Simon & Schuster

Each of the first three lettered sentences and the first five numbered sentences contains a phrase with inappropriate denotations or connotations. Each of the other sentences contains a phrase that is too general or abstract. Revise accordingly. Examples:

Mahatma Gandhi is ~~notorious~~. (denotation / connotation)
famous

Meet me ~~this afternoon~~. (general / abstract)
at 3:47 p.m.

a. The gardener's hide was sunburned. (denotation/connotation)

b. The basketball player is lofty. (denotation/connotation)

c. Her perfume has a wonderful aroma. (denotation/connotation)

d. I bought a car. (general/abstract)

e. The cheeseburger cost a lot of money. (general/abstract)

1. The customer politely demanded that I help her. (denotation/connotation)

2. I buy my groceries at the boutique. (denotation/connotation)

3. The professor commended us that we'd have a quiz soon. (denotation/connotation)

4. I clandestinely hid the present. (denotation/connotation)

5. Coach Jones eulogized the team for its good game. (denotation/connotation)

6. I read the book. (general/abstract)

7. I saw the movie. (general/abstract)

8. I want to complete my education. (general/abstract)

9. Candidate X supports family values. (general/abstract)

10. Candidate X also supports public transportation. (general/abstract)

11

11--Word Impact

© 1995 Simon & Schuster

Revise words with inappropriate impact in the following sentences.
Example:

My brother is in ~~a rehabilitation facility.~~ *prison.*

a. Bette Davis was an American actress who won an Academy Award for her work in

  Dangerous.

b. I think I'll flunk accounting.

c. My mother has a heart of gold.

d. The door wouldn't close because the carpenters had inserted it at variance with the

  instructions.

e. After attending the funeral, we went to the graveside ceremony in the memory garden.

1. We ain't done.

2. He is a bear in the forest on the football field, but a cream puff at home.

3. Chris Evert plays tennis with the methodical grace and patience of a lioness hunting its

  prey.

4. If I don't get a handle on these math problems, I'll be up the crick in math class.

5. The candidate misspoke herself.

6. He's happy as a lark and smart as a whip.

7. A person needs to be tough as nails to reach the top of the heap.

8. After all is said and done, far be it from me at this point in time to disagree.

9. This store sells adult entertainment.

10. Our forces bombed the position to neutralize the enemy forces.

12--Nonsexist Language

Revise sexist language in the following sentences. Example:

Operating a dragline is a ~~man-sized~~ hard job.

a. Jocelyn Elders is a lady doctor.

b. The Constitution gives every American the right to speak his mind.

c. The men in the room applauded.

d. All police officers should be honest.

e. Mike was a house husband; he cleaned, took care of the children, and cooked.

1. Before sending in the forms, a taxpayer should check his calculations.

2. Mr. Newman and his wife, Joanne Woodward, live in Westport, Connecticut.

3. When a driver is stopped for a traffic violation, she should be polite to the policeman.

4. Polyester is a man-made material.

5. All men should exercise regularly.

6. An elementary teacher has her hands full, since she works with so many giggling girls and rowdy boys.

7. Women who want to become better cooks should read this magazine.

8. My aunt, who works as an accountant, is a career girl.

9. The common man doesn't understand the treaty.

10. Men need to have extensive training before they can qualify to become pilots.

13

Review--Sentence and Word Options

Revise the following sentences for sentence and word options if necessary. Example:

In fact, ^T the player of baseball blinked the lashes of his eyes all day because he needed batting practice.

a. A stool pigeon is a pigeon who has a tendency to sit a lot.

b. After snakes have had a fight, they hiss and make up.

c. When Ted crossed poison ivy with a clover that had four leaves, he got a rash of good luck.

d. When Ted crossed a lion and a rodent of the family *Muridae*, he got a mighty mouse.

e. The creature that is gray in coloration and that stamps out jungle fires is named Smokey the Elephant.

1. Our representatives are debating the bill at the present time.

2. The bill expresses its author's wish to increase the speed limit.

3. Florida's capital is Tallahassee, and the capital of New Mexico is Santa Fe.

4. We left at the crack of dawn, so we could make the trip in one day.

5. President Kennedy and his wife Jacqueline were an attractive young couple in the White House.

6. The average voter would approve of reducing government waste.

7. Arthur Fiedler, who conducted the Boston Pops from 1930 to 1979, was notorious for mixing popular and classical music in his concerts.

8. The sky grew light, and the clouds in the east glowed many colors.

9. Because Vatican City has a total area of less than a fifth of a square mile, it is the world's smallest nation.

10. The Sistine Chapel and Saint Peter's Basilica are located in Vatican City.

14

13--Main and Auxiliary Verbs

Underline main verbs once and auxiliary verbs twice in the following sentences. Example:

Jane might talk to Mark.

a. Jimmy Carter was president from 1977 to 1981.

b. He defeated President Gerald Ford in the 1976 election.

c. President Ford would have been president again if President Carter would not have won the election.

d. President Carter was known for his informality.

e. Ronald Reagan became president in 1981.

1. In a democracy, power is vested in the people.

2. People in a democracy might rule directly.

3. More commonly, people in a democracy elect representatives.

4. These representatives rule for the people.

5. Some countries, such as Britain and Sweden, combine a democracy with a monarchy in their governments.

6. Alexandre Dumas wrote *The Three Musketeers*.

7. The novel is set in seventeenth-century France.

8. D'Artagnan is the central character in the novel.

9. He becomes a musketeer after he performs a series of daring deeds.

10. D'Artagnan is younger than the other musketeers.

13--Transitive and Intransitive Verbs

Underline transitive verbs once and intransitive verbs twice in the following sentences.   Example:

Jane <u>talked</u> to Mark.

a.   Jane talked slowly today.

b.   She spoke too rapidly when she gave her speech yesterday.

c.   The professor leaned forward and listened yesterday.

d.   I am happy that she spoke slowly.

e.   When I give speeches, I speak slowly.

1.   Christopher Marlowe wrote the sixteenth-century English play *Doctor Faustus.*

2.   In Goethe's *Faust*, Mephistopheles tempts Faust.

3.   Faust sells his soul to the powers of darkness.

4.   Charles Gounod's opera *Faust* is about the same story.

5.   Gounod wrote his opera in 1859.

6.   Susan B. Anthony worked for women's rights.

7.   She was an active abolitionist (anti-slavery reformer) before the Civil War.

8.   In 1869 she cofounded the National Woman Suffrage Association.

9.   Anthony is particularly famous for her work in women's suffrage, or right to vote.

10. She died in 1920.

13--Regular and Irregular Verbs

Revise verbs in the following sentences if necessary.   Example:

My shoes were suppose$_\wedge$to be polished.

a.   I dived off the high board.

b.   Have you ever dived off the high board?

c.   The water in the pool were cold today.

d.   I have grew stronger as a swimmer.

e.   I also have worked out on the weights three times a week for the last six months.

1.   My mother works as a police officer.

2.   She helped catch the burglar who was stealing jewelry.

3.   I'm glad they caught the burglar.

4.   I've also chose to become a police officer.

5.   The work should be challenging.

6.   Don be studying for the test in economics class.

7.   He have a good grade in the class right now.

8.   Getting a low grade in the class would hurt his grade point average.

9.   He rise early this morning to study.

10.   He has written an outline for each chapter in the textbook.

13--Irregular Verbs

Revise verbs in the following sentences if necessary.   Example:

I ~~fall~~ *fell* down the stairs yesterday.

a.   Have you swam in this pool?

b.   Haris has already read the newspaper.

c.   Please lie the books on your desk.

d.   Maria become frustrated when the door wouldn't open.

e.   Erwin wear a blue shirt yesterday.

1.   I slept well.

2.   Sarah brought the burette to the chemistry professor.

3.   Had you began to do the experiment?

4.   Sarah took two years of chemistry in high school.

5.   My grandfather has kept the picture all of these years.

6.   The bugler has already blew reveille.

7.   This is the house that Jack built.

8.   Have you lay the books on your desk?

9.   I am laying down to rest.

10. We should have written our reports earlier.

13--Verb Tense

Follow the directions in parentheses when revising the verbs in the following sentences.   Example:

saw
I see the sign.   (past)

a.   I walk.   (future perfect)

b.   I walk.   (past)

c.   I walk.   (past perfect progressive)

d.   I walk.   (present progressive)

e.   I walk.   (future progressive)

1.   They sing. (future perfect)

2.   They sing. (future progressive)

3.   They sing. (future perfect progressive)

4.   They sing. (future)

5.   They sing. (past)

6.   We sit. (present perfect)

7.   We sit. (present progressive)

8.   We sit. (present perfect progressive)

9.   We sit. (past perfect progressive)

10. We sit. (past)

13--Verb Tense, Voice, and Mood

Revise verbs in the following sentences if necessary. Examples:

The temperature has dropped since the clouds cover␣ed␣the sun.

If it ~~was~~ were sunny, we could go to the beach.

~~The seeing was done by me~~ I saw that the clouds covered the sun.

a. Joan of Arc was a French military leader in the fifteenth century who says that God spoke to her in voices.

b. Shortly after the army she led forced the English to end their siege of Orleans in 1429, she had the dauphin crowned Charles VII.

c. If Joan of Arc would have lived in the twentieth century, she probably would have been a religious or military leader.

d. I wish that time travel was possible, so I could meet her.

e. The meeting of Joan of Arc by me I would find interesting.

1. The planet Neptune was discovered in 1846.

2. Before Neptune's discovery, astronomers observes that the planet Uranus sometimes sped up and sometimes slowed down as it orbited the sun.

3. The astronomers theorizes that the gravitational pull of another planet caused this uneven movement.

4. They confirmed this theory by sighting Neptune.

5. The planet Neptune is named after the Roman god of the sea, Neptune; astronomers use his fishing spear, the trident, as the planet's symbol.

6. You would surely have won the election if you would have campaigned.

7. Dr. Chang will have helped many people recover by the time she retires.

8. If Dr. Chang was not going to retire next year, I would ask her to be my family physician.

9. Widespread infant immunization has virtually eliminated diphtheria as a disease in developed countries.

10. Unless we continue this program of infant immunization, diphtheria will again become a problem in these countries.

14--Singular and Plural Subjects

Underline singular subjects once and plural subjects twice in the following sentences. Example:

<u>Geronimo</u> was an Apache.

a. Gargoyles were used on many buildings during the Middle Ages.

b. A gargoyle is a sculpture depicting a grotesque or fantastic creature.

c. Often used to carry rainwater clear of a wall, gargoyles were used frequently on Gothic buildings.

d. The rainwater was normally expelled through the projecting mouth of a gargoyle.

e. At times, gargoyles were used simply for ornamentation.

1. Mercantilism was the main economic doctrine for several hundred years after the decline of feudalism.

2. A nation's wealth, in this doctrine, was mainly based on the amount of gold and silver in the nation's treasury.

3. Accumulating gold and silver bullion, establishing colonies, developing a strong merchant marine, and encouraging mining and industry were approaches nations used to develop favorable balances of trade.

4. All mercantilist countries shared a common goal: to achieve a surplus of exports over imports, in order to build the national wealth.

5. This doctrine encouraged European countries to develop colonial holdings in Asia, Africa, North America, and South America.

6. Hydrogen, the lightest chemical element, normally has as its atom one electron in orbit around one proton.

7. In fusion reactions in stars and in hydrogen bombs, hydrogen atoms combine to form helium atoms.

8. This fusion releases huge amounts of energy.

9. On earth, hydrogen is usually found as a gas.

10. Hydrogen is the most abundant element in the universe.

14--Subject-Verb Agreement

Revise the following sentences if subjects and verbs do not agree.
Example:

$\quad$ *are*

They ~~is~~ talking.

a. He usually rides the bus to work.

b. Some of the buses is overheated.

c. Across the street is a bus stop.

d. The worst part of riding a bus are the waiting.

e. Seventy-five cents are the current bus fare.

1. Chief among his good qualities are his sense of humor.

2. The members of the basketball team are tall.

3. One of the problems at the university are inadequate parking.

4. Liver and onions are not one of my favorite foods.

5. Each class I wanted to take were closed.

6. Sarah and her two karate instructors are very disciplined.

7. Neither Mike nor his two roommates is very ambitious.

8. Each of the lawns need to be mowed.

9. There are five cups on the table.

10. The marching band has 117 students in it.

15--Identifying Pronouns

Underline pronouns in the following sentences.   Example:

I said it myself.

a.   Give it to me.

b.   Give the ball to me.

c.   Would anybody like to help me eat the pizza?

d.   This is Mike's jacket.

e.   Please pass the salt.

1.   Mercury is a silvery-white metallic element; it is poisonous.

2.   Although it is a metal, mercury is liquid at room temperatures.

3.   Mercury's melting point is about minus 39 C.

4.   Mercury is also called quicksilver.

5.   While they were working with it in the laboratory, Heather and Samita handled the mercury very carefully.

6.   The planet Mercury is the planet that is closest to the sun.

7.   It is named after Mercury, who was the fleet-footed messenger of the Roman gods.

8.   Mercury goes around the sun in eighty-eight days.

9.   We can occasionally see Mercury as a morning or an evening star.

10. This is a planet photographed by Mariner 10 in 1975.

15--Pronoun Antecedents

Revise the following sentences if necessary.   Example:

~~Each of~~ T̂he students opened their book.

a.   Gilbert and Sullivan collaborated on many operettas; Gilbert wrote the lyrics and

dialogue, and he wrote the music.

b.   I like to study biological trivia; that is my major.

c.   In Montana they say that the cold keeps the riffraff out.

d.   Either the compact disc player or the loudspeaker needs its wiring repaired.

e.   The band put away their instruments.

1.   I waited at the bus stop until it came.

2.   Food poisoning might result if you handle food improperly.

3.   Calamity Jane, who boasted of her adventures as a Pony Express rider and a scout,

was a sharpshooter.

4.   The umbrella that I want to buy is on sale.

5.   The dog wagged its tail.

6.   My father and mother went to Louisville for their wedding anniversary.

7.   Each of the students wrote their own paper.

8.   The family opened their presents at Christmas.

9.   The audience settled into their seats as the curtain rose.

10. Every member of the audience were happy.

15--Pronoun Case

Revise pronouns in the following sentences if necessary. Example:
    He
~~Him~~ **and I are on the football team.**

a. John, Sarah, and me ate the pizza.

b. The manager gave the box to Maria and me.

c. We orchestra members practice frequently.

d. Who attended the concert?

e. The coach praised my friend and myself for our hard work.

1. She and I went to the concert.

2. The concert bored her and I.

3. She and myself were bored by the concert.

4. Our professor expects him to win the scholarship.

5. The car's driver was I.

6. The car was mine.

7. Whomever told you that?

8. Rising book prices are a problem all of us students face.

9. To whom should I speak about admission to law school?

10. He told his stupid jokes to my sister and myself.

16--Adjectives

Underline adjectives in the following sentences. Example:

She felt happy.

a. The old car is rusty.

b. I drove the rusty old car.

c. The car is old and rusty.

d. The car--old, rusty, decrepit--belongs to my grandfather.

e. It holds many memories for him.

1. Members of the winning team are usually happier than members of the losing team.

2. Unblanched celery is greener than blanched celery.

3. We bought the most expensive meal at the restaurant.

4. Betty's horse is strong.

5. Betty's horse is stronger than Mike's horse.

6. Betty's horse is the strongest horse on the team.

7. Betty's horse runs rapidly.

8. You look well.

9. You write well.

10. He walked slowly.

28

16--Adverbs

Underline adverbs in the following sentences. Example:

The cook felt <u>unusually</u> creative <u>today</u>.

a.   The fireplace was very hot.

b.   The high temperature for that day was twenty below zero.

c.   We regularly fed the fireplace huge chunks of ash.

d.   The wind rattled the windowpanes and swirled the snow.

e.   The bare trees swayed.

1.   Mary's performance in the basketball game was truly memorable.

2.   She ran more rapidly than the other center.

3.   She also jumped higher than the other center.

4.   Mary played memorably.

5.   Mary played well.

6.   The family room is the most frequently used room in our house.

7.   We use the basement the least frequently.

8.   Today the family room was insufferably hot.

9.   The thermostat apparently was broken.

10. The service technician is working on the thermostat now.

16--Using Adjectives and Adverbs

Revise adjectives and adverbs in the following sentences if necessary. Examples:

The careless~~ly~~ chauffeur drove the car.

This cheesecake is less tasty than regular cheesecake because it contains
fewer
~~less~~ calories than regular cheesecake.

a.   The dog barked loudly.

b.   The dog barked very loudly.

c.   We didn't have no way to quiet the dog.

d.   The dog is noisy.

e.   My next door neighbors' dog is the noisiest dog in the neighborhood.

1.   Beth is happy.

2.   Beth ran rapid.

3.   She ran good.

4.   Beth ran more rapidly than the other athletes.

5.   She ran the best race she has ever run.

6.   We all think happily about that race.

7.   The trophy she won looks well in her room.

8.   Even when she was in grade school, Beth was swift.

9.   She was swifter than her brother.

10. She was the most swiftest runner in sixth grade.

17--Sentence Fragments

If an exercise contains either a sentence fragment and one complete sentence or two fragments, combine the fragment and sentence or the fragments into one sentence. If an exercise contains two complete sentences, go to the next exercise. Example:

Albert Schweitzer, the German theologian, musician, and physician, received many awards, *including the Nobel Prize for peace,* for his work as a humanitarian and missionary in Africa. ~~Including the Nobel Prize for peace.~~

a.   What is the difference between a cat and a sentence? A cat has claws at the end of its paws, and a sentence has a pause at the end of its clause.

b.   In Modern English *girl* denotes a female child. In Middle English, from the thirteenth to the fifteenth century, *girl* denoted a child of either sex.

c.   The word *balkanization* derives from the name of the Balkan Peninsula, which was divided into several small nations. In the early twentieth century.

d.   Bacteria at times present in incorrectly canned or preserved foods cause botulism, a type of food poisoning. Which is often fatal if not treated properly.

e.   Melanie, in the film *Gone With The Wind.* Played by Olivia de Havilland.

1.   Simit. A big dark ring of sesame-covered Turkish bread.

2.   Turkish salads often contain vegetables which Americans associate with Italy. These salads also often contain ingredients which Americans associate with countries farther east than Turkey, including red-pepper paste, walnut sauce, and cracked wheat.

3.   A dozen words for *peat.* In the Irish language.

4.   Snow hardens into glaciers. Glaciers cover ten percent of the earth's land mass.

5.   Greenland icecaps. About two miles thick in places.

6.   In the late 1970s. Scott Olson designed many of the improvements in in-line skates that have made them become so popular since.

7. Tofu. Made from soybeans.

8. Ginger Rogers was an actress and dancer.

9. In the early seventeenth century Henry Hudson explored the Hudson River.

10. In computer science a bit is the smallest unit of information. The word is a blend of b(inary) and (dig)it.

18--Comma Splices and Fused Sentences

Revise the following exercises to eliminate comma splices and fused sentences. Example:

I bought the tickets,$_\wedge$we attended the concert.
and

a.   Auto companies around the world are now producing prototypes for vastly different cars than cars now on the road; new technologies have made these prototypes possible.

b.   A huge engine probably powers a 1995 car, a 2005 car might be powered by a small engine that produces energy to run electric motors for independently powering each wheel.

c.   This small engine might be augmented by a carbon-fiber flywheel that will store energy recovered from braking or from descending hills.

d.   Electric cars now carry batteries weighing nearly half a ton, but this small engine for producing electricity might weigh only a couple of hundred pounds.

e.   Different types of engines, including gas turbines, could reduce this weight significantly; these types of engines are now being developed.

1.   Some people frown on gambling but many phrases in American English originally were associated with gambling.

2.   President Harry Truman kept a sign that said "The buck stops here" on his desk; the phrase was originally used in poker games in the 1800s.

3.   In the West players often passed a knife with a handle made of buck horn around the table to show who had the deal, as a result, the buck stopped at the dealer of the game.

4.   _Passing the buck_ had a literal origin; it meant passing the knife (and the deal).

5. White, red, and blue chips are used for betting in poker, with blue chips being the most valuable; similarly, blue-chip stocks on the stock market are normally those that are most stable, secure, and, often, most valuable.

6. Italian cheeses come in a variety of types; not all are hard cheeses for grating.

7. Italian mozzarella is made from water-buffalo milk, and it has a short shelf life so it is unlike the mozzarella Americans put on pizzas.

8. Fontina is a mild and relatively soft cheese, suitable for slicing or spreading, but aged provolone is a sharp and hard cheese, suitable for grating.

9. Fontina that is produced high in the Alps in the summer has a higher fat content than ordinary fontina, this extra fat makes the summer fontina highly prized.

10. Mozzarella made of water-buffalo milk has a shelf life of several days, provolone may be aged two years before it is ready.

19--Shifts and Derailed Sentences
© 1995 Simon & Schuster

Revise the following sentences if necessary. Example:

When ~~a person~~ People visits Yellowstone Park, they should do a lot of walking.

a. I enjoy reading my horoscope, but you really wonder if it's ever true.

b. According to Mae West, "Too much of a good thing can be wonderful."

c. By standing inside the penalty area allows a soccer goalie to handle the ball.

d. Arthur Ashe was the first black winning the Wimbledon men's singles tennis title.

e. One reason that August, 1961, is an important month is because the Berlin Wall was erected then.

1. A private citizen may legally make an arrest if they have observed a crime or have reasonable cause to believe a crime has been committed.

2. The more a person studies a foreign language, the better they should expect to speak it.

3. Many students expect to eventually find jobs in their major fields, but they anticipate probably some problems in doing so.

4. The majority of the students in my political science class identified three main goals for government: to balance the budget, to reduce crime, and to protect the environment.

5. People who are physically fit are better athletes.

6. During the first opening-day game in Yankee Stadium, Babe Ruth hit a three-run homer.

7. The purpose of the George Washington Bridge was built to span the Hudson River.

8. Edward R. Murrow's outstanding characteristic as a newscaster was his dramatic factuality.

9. Canada is where there is the most coastline in a country.

10. Prohibition was the period that began and lasted from 1920 to 1933 during which the manufacture and sale of alcoholic beverages was forbidden in the United States.

20--Misplaced and Dangling Modifiers

Revise misplaced and dangling modifiers in the following sentences.
Example:

completely

How the police officer^subdued the violent suspect ~~completely~~ amazed me.

a. The shepherd's dog ran loudly barking toward the sheep.

b. The shepherd signaled her dog to herd the sheep, anxious to go home.

c. The shepherd wanted her dog to quickly herd the sheep home and to leave no stragglers.

d. The shepherd just had bought her dog from a neighboring rancher.

e. Until home, the dog herded the sheep diligently.

1. Stolen from our room last week, my roommate saw our stereo equipment in the pawn shop.
2. My roommate saw our stereo equipment in the pawn shop that was stolen from our room last week.
3. We immediately called the police.
4. Two officers arrived and talked with the owner of the pawn shop, determined to solve the crime.
5. The officers wanted to quickly solve the crime.
6. We never could have talked so persuasively with the owner.
7. Unwilling to believe that her nephew had stolen the stereo, a mistake was the explanation the owner of the pawn shop gave.
8. My roommate and I told the officers that we knew her nephew slightly, but that we had not given him our stereo equipment.
9. Engraved on each piece of equipment, our Social Security numbers proved the equipment was ours.
10. After his sentencing, the nephew was sure by January that he would be on parole.

Review--Correct Grammar

Revise the following sentences if necessary. Example:

Batman brush_∧**with toothpaste to prevent bat breath.**

a. The big hill knew the little hill wasn't telling the truth because it was only a bluff.

b. If everyone in the country would buy a pink car, would we have a pink carnation?

c. He said what do you call a conceited woman?--"Mimi."

d. "The reason that I nicknamed him 'Blair,'" Tod said, "is because he honks his car horn so often."

e. Since he likes to ring doorbells, we called him "Buzz."

1. She speaking Spanish to her friends.

2. Have you chose the book you want to read?

3. Show me a good mudder, and I'll show you a horse who can win a race in the rain.

4. The first issue of *Playboy* cost fifty cents.

5. Mosquitoes and flies are health hazards, since they both carry disease.

6. Kathy Whitworth was the first woman golfer to earn a million dollars.

7. She played golf good.

8. This sandwich is less tasty because, without the butter, it contains less calories.

9. I like this sandwich, which contains butter and mayonnaise, better than the other sandwiches on the tray.

10. The sandwich with butter and mayonnaise is the most fattening sandwich on the tray.

21--Comma Use
©1995 Simon & Schuster

Add or delete commas in the following sentences if necessary. Example:
The seven deadly sins are anger, covetousness (greed), envy, gluttony, lust,
pride, and sloth.

a.   Myopia, or nearsightedness, is a visual defect.

b.   For myopic people distant objects appear blurred.

c.   A myopic person's eyes focus light in front of the retina, but a non-myopic person's
     eyes focus light on the retina.

d.   A person who wears glasses or contact lenses may be myopic.

e.   Myopia therefore, is a visual defect which ordinarily can be corrected.

1.   The word, *deadline* was first used during the Civil War.

2.   In Andersonville, the Confederate POW camp, guards could shoot prisoners who
      crossed a boundary line running several feet inside the outer wall.

3.   A deadline originally was a physical line not to be crossed, but now, nearly, 150 years
      later, it is a line in time not to be crossed.

4.   "For truth there is no deadline" wrote Heywood Broun.

5.   *The Nation* published Broun's article on December 30, 1939.

6.   Writers who can meet deadlines.

7.   Millions of people took Thalidomide as a sedative during the 1950s and the 1960s.

8.   Most of these people suffered no ill effects, but at least 10,000 women who took
     Thalidomide during their pregnancies gave birth to physically deformed babies.

9.   The deformities included missing or stunted limbs: hands at the elbows, two fingers
     instead of five, and flippers rather than legs.

10. Gilla Kaplan, M.D., discovered in 1989 how Thalidomide affects the immune system
     and realized that the drug might be useful in fighting a number of diseases.

38

22--Comma Misuse

Add or delete commas in the following sentences if necessary. Example:

Light heavyweight boxers weigh between 160, and 175 pounds.

a. Although, Canada's area is 4,000,000 square miles, its population is under 30,000,000 people.

b. Canada produces large quantities of wheat, and beef.

c. Much of Canada lies in the harsh northern latitudes.

d. Copper, gold, nickel, and zinc, are some of the abundant minerals in Canada's reserves.

e. Winnipeg, Manitoba, is home for one of the best ballet companies in North America.

1. Miss Muffet sat on a tuffet, and ate curds and whey.

2. Miss Muffet apparently wanted to sit on the tuffet, but, a spider frightened her away.

3. Because the spider sat by Miss Muffet, Miss Muffet left the tuffet.

4. Miss Muffet, who was little, sat on a tuffet.

5. Little, Miss Muffet sat on a tuffet.

6. Elvis Presley, who was nicknamed "The King," was born in 1935.

7. Elvis Presley was probably a more important singer, than Buddy Holly.

8. Since television executives in the 1950s thought his hip gyrations too suggestive to broadcast, cameras recorded him only from his waist up.

9. Presley has become, a legend in popular culture.

10. Elvis Presley's hit records include "Heartbreak Hotel," "Hound Dog," and "Don't Be Cruel."

21 and 22--Unnecessary Commas

Delete commas in the following sentences if necessary. Example:

The oak tree that I planted two years ago/ is growing.

a. The large, friendly, restless crowd waited for the music.

b. They knew they would hear three popular backup singers.

c. Organic farmers, who do not use chemicals, rely on other methods to control pests.

d. The game was televised on February 4, 1995.

e. We drove 1,200, miles on Friday.

1. The child held the spoon, intently.

2. The, small restless crowd waited for the fireworks display.

3. The display featured, many of the same fireworks used every year.

4. The song called, "Slow Sailing," displays Mickey Hart's talents at their finest.

5. When the professor talked about the next test, all of the students listened.

6. I laughed, and cried during the movie.

7. I laughed, cried, and then laughed again during the movie.

8. I laughed, because the movie was funny.

9. Because the movie was sad, I cried.

10. He walked, against the traffic, rather than with it.

23--Semicolon Use

Revise the following sentences if necessary by adding or deleting semicolons, by substituting semicolons for other marks of punctuation, or by substituting other marks of punctuation for semicolons. Example:

We biked 80 miles today, the workout was superb.

a. The committee included Jim Smith, the new accountant; Sarah Jones, the coordinator of the advertising division; and Tracy Youngblood, the director of public relations.

b. "For tomorrow," the professor in my Bible as Literature class said, "read Genesis 1:1-10; Psalm 23:1-6; and Job 1:1-10."

c. Stephen A. Douglas was a nineteenth-century political leader who ran twice against Abraham Lincoln.

d. Douglas won the race against Lincoln to be senator from Illinois in 1858, he lost the race against Lincoln for the presidency in 1860.

e. The two men debated slavery in 1858; these debates are still remembered as the Lincoln-Douglas Debates.

1. The supervisor said, "If you're going to get this job done; you'll need to apply some more elbow grease."

2. The supervisor said, "The inspector will come tomorrow; we're doing everything by the book this week."

3. While working on the cleaning crew, we scrubbed pots, pans, and sinks; washed floors, walls, and doors; and dusted all of the furniture.

4. The inspector arrived early; although we had finished our cleaning early as well.

5. The inspector praised the supervisor for a job well done; but the supervisor didn't say anything about the inspectors' praise when we came to work the next day.

6. Shakespeare wrote *Antony and Cleopatra*; *As You Like It*; *Hamlet; Julius Caesar*; *King Lear*; and *Macbeth*.

7 Born in Stratford-on-Avon, Shakespeare spent most of his career in London.

8. He worked as an actor, playwright, and manager of the Globe Theater.

9. He spent his retirement back in Stratford; where he died in 1616.

10. The *First Folio*, the earliest collected edition of his plays, was published in 1623.

24--Colon Use

©1995 Simon & Schuster

Revise the following sentences if necessary by adding or deleting colons, by substituting colons for other marks of punctuation, or by substituting other marks of punctuation for colons. Example:

Of this I am sure, you will have the car no more than three months before it gives you trouble.

a. Imitating the title of Stephen W. Hawking's book *A Brief History of Time: From the Big Bang to Black Holes*, my brother called his paper *A Brief History of My Time in the Chemistry Lab: From Unknown Chemicals to Unknown Chemicals*.

b. I woke up at 6,45 in the morning.

c. After my brother and his friends have been in the kitchen, I know what the refrigerator will look like: empty.

d. During the 1980's, the United States failed to: reduce the national debt, win the war against drugs, or win the war against cancer.

e. The chaplain read Mark 1, 1.

1. During the 1980's, the United States failed to meet three long-standing national goals: reducing the national debt, winning the war against drugs, and winning the war against cancer.

2. I will never forget the first time I tried to ski: I fell in the middle of the slope, and I struggled for twenty minutes to get up.

3. The Queen of Hearts, in Lewis Carroll's *Alice's Adventures in Wonderland*, has an easy but gruesome answer whenever anyone bothers her: "Off with her head! Off with his head!"

4. If you really want to be educated, you need to do only three things: read, read, and read.

5. Boston maintains one of the few great ballparks left: Fenway Park.

6. In Richard Brinsley Sheridan's play *The Rivals*, Mrs. Malaprop says: "He is the very *pineapple* of politeness."

7. She means: *pinnacle*.

8. A malapropism today means: a funny misuse of a word by confusing it with one that sounds somewhat like it.

9. When my roommate and I went to see *The Rivals*, we laughed more loudly than other people in the audience.

10. People turned and looked: at us.

23 and 24--Semicolon and Colon Use
©1995 Simon & Schuster

Revise the following sentences if necessary by adding or deleting semicolons or colons, by substituting semicolons or colons for other marks of punctuation, or by substituting other marks of punctuation for semicolons or colons. Example:

The Parthenon was built between 447 and 432 B.C.; it served as a model for much ancient Greek and Roman architecture.

The Acropolis is the site of famous ruins, including the Parthenon.

a. Although Steven Spielberg established his reputation by making adventure films; he made *Schindler's List*, based on historic fact, in 1993.

b. These adventure films include: *Raiders of the Lost Ark* (1981) and *E.T.* (1982).

c. Spielberg was known for his adventure films; nevertheless, he earned critical acclaim and popular success with *Schindler's List*.

d. He has now established a non-profit foundation to videotape and preserve interviews with Holocaust survivors; he plans to record 50,000 interviews by 1994.

e. The project is projected to be expensive: $65 million.

1. Body language includes: gestures and eye contact.

2. The American gesture for "okay" involves forming a circle with the forefinger and the thumb; this gesture means "zero" in France.

3. The American gesture for "okay" has various meanings in other cultures: "zero" in France, "money" in Japan, and a vulgarity in Brazil.

4. When they are working in foreign countries, business people need to understand that body language has various meanings, depending on culture; otherwise, these people may offend potential customers.

5. Looking someone in the eye means honesty in the United States and Canada; in most Asian and Latin American countries, it might mean aggression or ill breeding.

6. Asian business people tend to prefer: brief or no handshakes, sitting side by side during negotiations, and long negotiations.

7. Business people in the Middle East usually stand about two feet apart when talking; business people in the United States and Canada usually stand about five feet apart.

8. The chaplain read Genesis 1:1.

9. Math majors outnumbered other science majors in the calculus class by 2;1.

10. The marathon runner crossed the finish line at 3:15:10.

25 and 26--End Punctuation and Apostrophes

Add or delete end punctuation or apostrophes in the following sentences if necessary and, after doing so, revise the sentences if necessary. Example:

My roommate, who's^e talents do not include cooking, makes ~~very good (?)~~ meals/ that a hungry dog might like.

a. Mexico's area is 761,000 square miles

b. Its population in 1993 was 84.4 million.

c. Mexico's capital, Mexico City, is it's largest city.

d. Mexico Citys population in 1992 was nearly nine million, while New York City's population in 1992 was about seven million.

e. Mexico City's larger than New York City.

1. I asked, "Do you want to go to Mexico City?"

2. My friend shouted, "Yes!"

3. My friend is a quiet (?) person.

4. Gilbert and Sullivan's operettas include *H.M.S. Pinafore* and *The Mikado*.

5. Gilbert and Sullivan wrote this operetta in the late 1800s.

6. The music is difficult, so only experienced singers' can sing the lead roles.

7. The price sticker on the new car contained too many 9's.

8. I'm astonished by all of the new cars prices.

9. My parents' car insurance costs less than mine.

10. My business's profits need to increase before I will buy a car.

27--Quotation Marks

Add or delete quotation marks and revise other punctuation marks in the following sentences if necessary, and revise any tired or inappropriate language enclosed in quotation marks in the following sentences. Example:

In a speech he gave in Detroit on June 23, 1963, Martin Luther King, Jr., said, "If a man hasn't discovered something that he will die for, he isn't fit to live⌣. "

a. Have you read Dr. King's Letter from Birmingham Jail"?

b. In the introductory notes to her compact disc *Mas Canciones*, Linda Ronstadt writes, "Since I was a young child, I have loved and admired the traditional music of Mexico in all its wondrous diversity".

c. Many people confuse lie and lay.

d. The proposed "changes" are actually a return to previous practices.

e. Thomas Gray's poem "Elegy Written in a Country Churchyard" contains the line, "The paths of glory lead but to the grave."

1. In his "Inaugural Address," John F. Kennedy challenged all Americans by saying, "Ask not what your country can do for you; ask what you can do for your country."

2. In his "Inaugural Address, John F. Kennedy challenged Americans to serve their country, rather that expecting their country to serve them.

3. In "Whom says so?" in *The Nation,* June 8, 1985, Calvin Trillin writes, 'As far as I'm concerned, "whom" is a word that was invented to make everyone sound like a butler'.

4. I asked Mary, Why did you name your pickup "Buck?"

5. "Because, Mary said, people pass it so often."

6. I like the Latin proverb *Ars longa, vita brevis* (life is short, art is long").

7. Chaucer translated the proverb as, "The life so short, the art so long to learn."

8. Have you read Louise Erdrich's poem "Dear John Wayne"?

9. The scholarship I received from the service club was "only a drop in the bucket," but I "thanked the club president from the bottom of my heart."

10. "Defamation" is a false and malicious statement, communicated to others, that injures a person's reputation; defamation in writing is "slander."

28--Other Punctuation Marks

Add or delete punctuation marks in the following sentences if necessary. Example:

The Catcher in the Rye **was published during the same general period in** /American/ **literature as** *Catch-22.*

a. Pandora opened the box that Zeus had given her--so the story goes--and let loose all the evils and miseries that now afflict humanity.

b. Some bacteria those that live in the digestive tract and aid digestion, for example are beneficial to humans.

c. Mark Twain's *The Adventures of Huckleberry Finn* contains lines I like, such as "There was [sic] things he stretched, but mainly he told the truth."

d. In her poem "Chahinkapa Zoo," Louise Erdrich writes about the frustration wild animals in zoos must feel; the poem begins "It is spring. Even here/ The bears emerge from poured caverns./ Already their cubs have been devoured/ by the feather-footed lynx caged next door."

e. Erdrich's zoo is a nasty place in which the bears' "cubs have been devoured / by the . . . Lynx caged next door."

1. They love Italian food--minestrone soup, pasta, and grated hard cheese.

2. I know that Maria--the painter--does good work.

3. The agenda for the Midtown Car Club meeting includes 1 whether we should rent the garage, 2 recruiting new members, and 3 whether we should buy new tires at this time.

4. The Midtown Car Club would like to buy eight (8) tires.

5. This circuit on the computer is hard-wired (built to do a specific job), so it needs no program to function properly.

6. Some fears, (of falling, for example) appear to be genetically transmitted, or hard-wired into some creatures' brains.

7. Rebuilding the pier (waves destroyed most of the original.) took two months.

8. Only about 1/10 of the original pier was left standing.

9. The spiritual begins "Joshua fit [sic] the battle of Jericho, / Jericho, Jericho, / Joshua fit the battle of Jericho, / And the walls came a-tumblin' [sic] down."

10. I sang "Joshua fit the battle of Jericho, / Jericho, Jericho . . . ."

Review--Punctuation
©1995 Simon & Schuster

Revise punctuation in the following sentences if necessary. Example:

The one cannibal said, "I don't like your friend," and the second cannibal
said, "That's okay, just eat the vegetables."

a. People call her "Sue" because she is always taking people to court.

b. Jimmy is the man who breaks into houses

c. Chlorophyll makes plants green.

d. I read Psalm 23-1:3.

e. The Library of Congress, which was built in 1897, contains 327 miles of
    bookshelves.

1. According to a study published in 1980 in *Public Health Reports*, the survival rate for
    people who were recovering from heart attacks and who owned pets was higher than
    the survival rate for people without pets.

2. The study, limited though it was, seems to show that having a pet helps a person
    recover from a heart attack.

3. The mortality rate for people owning pets' was about 1/3 that of the people who did
    not own pets.

4. One possible explanation is that: the pets helped their owners relax.

5. Staff members at many nursing homes, prisons, and mental institutions now bring in
    pets to interact with people who are depressed, lonely, and unhappy.

6. Barbra Streisand, and Katharine Hepburn, tied for the best actress Oscar in 1968.

7. A person, when drawing a bow, uses three fingers.

8. January 1, 2001, will be on a Monday.

9. Astronomy is a scientific study; astrology, on the other hand, is not.

10. The month of March is named after the planet Mars.

29--Capitals

Add or delete capitals in the following sentences if necessary. Example:

In her book *The Warrior Woman*, Maxine Hong Kingston writes, "~~my~~ M aunt haunts me--her ghost drawn to me because now, after fifty years of neglect, I alone devote pages of paper to her, though not origamied into houses and clothes."

a.   Anwar Sadat was President of Egypt from 1970 until 1981.

b.   President Sadat shared the 1978 Nobel Peace Prize with Prime Minister Menachem Begin of Israel.

c.   When Sadat visited Israel in 1977, Golda Meir told him that she "Never did anything alone. Whatever was accomplished in this country was accomplished collectively."

d.   Sadat was assassinated by Islamic extremists in 1981.

e.   Three of the main factors that caused the assassination include (1) Inadequate security for Sadat, (2) Anger over his agreements with Israel, and (3) Arab nationalism.

1.   If threatened, a horned toad has a unique defense: it squirts blood at its adversaries from a place near its eyes.

2.   In addition to the spines on their bodies, horned toads have four forms of defense: (1) Blending into the environment, (2) Inflating to appear larger, (3) Running away, and (4) Squirting blood.

3.   "Horned toads," the biology professor explained, "are actually lizards, not toads."

4.   Horned toads are native to the band of land extending from Southern British Columbia to Northern Guatemala.

5.   Horned toads, like other reptiles, are Ectotherms--their body temperature rises and falls with the temperature of their environment.

6.   George S. Patton, Jr., was an American General during World War II.

7. Patton led the Third Army's sweep across France and into Germany.

8. Patton, known for his forceful leadership, was nicknamed "Old Blood and Guts."

9. "I have come to consider myself," Patton wrote in his diary, "as a sort of chip floating down a river of destiny."

10. Patton is an important figure in recent History.

30--Italics

Either add or remove underlining (italic type) or quotation marks in the following sentences if necessary. Example:

I frequently eat bean ~~burritos~~ *burritos* for lunch.

a. In his book *Blue Highways*, William Least Heat Moon published an account of the trip he took around the United States in an old van he called "Ghost Dancer."

b. We traveled in a *Boeing 747*.

c. Is this a 3 or an 8?

d. She read about it in *Newsweek*.

e. Chaucer's *Canterbury Tales* is a set of stories told in verse.

1. Zora Neale Hurston's "Their Eyes were Watching God" is now generally considered to be one the best American novels written in the twentieth century.

2. Georgia O'Keeffe's painting The Winter Road, 1963 is reproduced in full color in the book *Georgia O'Keeffe*.

3. Alice Walker published her novel "The Color Purple" in 1982.

4. Is the U.S.S. *Missouri* a battleship?

5. Marilyn Monroe appeared in the movie Some Like It Hot.

6. Linda Ronstadt performs the song "Tata Dios" on her compact disc "Mas Canciones."

7. Do you like sushi?

8. I nearly wrote that the singer "brought the house down," but I didn't--I wanted to avoid using a cliché.

9. Do you read the Los Angeles Times?

10. Have you heard any of Verdi's *operas*?

31--Abbreviations

Revise the abbreviations and punctuation marks in the following sentences if necessary. Example:

The concert will begin at 7:30 p.m. /

a. While discussing the pessimism so pervasive in the fourteenth century (A.D. 1300-1399), Barbara Tuchman writes in her book *A Distant Mirror*, "Death is not treated poetically as the soul's flight to reunion with God; it is a skeleton grinning at the vanity of life."

b. Each new bomber will cost $56 million.

c. Dr. Jocelyn Elders, M.D., who served the U.S. as surgeon general in 1992-93, grew up the daughter of a sharecropper in Ark.

d. Desiderius Erasmus was a leader during the Reformation who advocated studying the literature of ancient Greece and Rome, increasing personal piety, changing the Catholic Church, etc.

e. I wrote to my friend at 0000 Whatever Road, Minneapolis, MN.

1. My job starts at 8:30 A.M.

2. Julius Caesar introduced the Julian calendar in Rome in B.C. 46.

3. A yard equals 36 in.

4. Water freezes at thirty-two degrees Fahrenheit.

5. Col. David H. Hackworth writes frequently about the US military.

6. Richard Rodriguez, Ph.D., published *Days of Obligation* in 1993.

7. Rodriguez frequently appears as an essayist on the PBS program *The MacNeil-Lehrer News Hour*.

8. The Transco Tower, in Houston, TX, was designed by the famous American architect Philip Johnson.

9. J. Edgar Hoover served as director of the FBI from 1924 until 1972.

10. Please send the bill to Oak St. NW, Somewhere, NJ.

32--Numbers

Revise numbers in the following sentences if necessary.   Example:

Nineteen ninety-four

~~1994~~ was a good year.

a.   Barbara Bush was born in 1925.

b.   World War II ended in Europe on May 8, 1945.

c.   Uranium's melting point is 1,132 degrees C, and its boiling point is three thousand

eight hundred and eighteen degrees C.

d.   If there is an emergency, dial 911.

e.   Let's meet at 4:00 p.m.

1.   You'll find Table C on page 36.

2.   We sold only 1 pair of shoes in five days.

3.   I live at fifteen Elm Street.

4.   We'll meet at 3 o'clock.

5.   We'll meet at 3 in the afternoon.

6.   I've written 3-quarters of my paper.

7.   1921 is the year in which Nancy Reagan was born.

8.   A straight flush is ranked above four of a kind in poker.

9.   An ounce is 1/16 of a pound.

10.   A pound equals 453.592 grams.

33--Hyphens

Revise the hyphens in the following sentences if necessary. Example:

The final test will be all-inclusive.

a.   When we saw the shower scene in Hitchcock's *Psycho*, we all screamed.

b.   John Wayne always played self-reliant characters.

c.   Each of the graduated bowls that make a glass harmonica will produce a bell-like tone

     of a particular pitch when you press your finger to its moistened rim.

d.   The play director asked all cast members to re-dress for a group picture.

e.   The more-expensive coat is the better-looking coat.

1.   A short tempered umpire officiated at our baseball game.

2.   A pint is one-half of a quart.

3.   The ill prepared teacher was unable to conduct one full fifty-minute class all week.

4.   The teacher does not deserve a full-week's pay.

5.   The new overpass allows a clearance of two feet for semitrailers.

6.   The Milky Way is 50,000 light years in diameter.

7.   President-elect Jones spoke to us.

8.   Anti-intellectual students will not enjoy Ms. Smith's class.

9.   A toaster running for one hour will normally use one kilowatt hour of electricity.

10. The Smiths are a happily married couple.

34--Spelling Plurals

Correct misspelled words in the following sentences. Example:

My brother and my sister are both coach̬s.

a. Carl's legs are sunburned.

b. He was at two beachs yesterday.

c. He wore a shirt with long sleeves, but he wore swim trunks.

d. He wore shoes, so his feet are fine.

e. Carl is one of my brother-in-laws.

1. Did the children go out to play?

2. Do your data support your conclusion?

3. I keep the syllabi for all of my classes in this folder.

4. We ate three bowls of rice.

5. We saw a herd of elks when we were at the zoo.

6. We also saw three giraffes.

7. Did you rake the leaves?

8. I have three notebooks in my desk.

9. I paid my taxs early.

10. We are all alumni of Central High School.

34--Adding Suffixes and Spelling *ie, ei* Words

© 1995 Simon & Schuster

Correct misspelled words in the following sentences. Example:

In my opinion, fast food will never super~~c~~ede food made at home.

a.   The teacher spoke sharply.

b.   I beleive I will have my hair cut.

c.   Did you paint the cieling?

d.   When did they begin requiring jacket and tie in the restaurant?

e.   The company employed more people last year.

1.   The motorcycle cost eight thousand dollars.

2.   My neighbor bought it.

3.   She will likely not ride it in the fields.

4.   I find myself liking to read more than I did when I was in high school.

5.   I have a strong drive to succede.

6.   My roommate tries to solve all problems logically.

7.   Have you fried the potatoes?

8.   I hope not, since I'm trying to lose weight.

9.   I prefer iether boiled or baked food.

10. Have you taken a science class yet?

34--Spelling Homonyms

Correct misspelled words in the following sentences. Example:

I ate to$\overset{o}{\wedge}$many potato chips.

a.   The bride and groom walked down the isle.

b.   I accept the invitation.

c.   We went to the state fare.

d.   Have you seen the television program?

e.   It is better to recycle paper, rather than waisting it.

1.   My mother is principal at an elementary school.

2.   Who's hat is this?

3.   Is it your hat?

4.   Did you meet the visitors?

5.   We past the car.

6.   Did you see the lightening?

7.   It's been raining for three hours.

8.   We fed the bare in the zoo.

9.   I would like to by the chair buy next weak.

10. Should I dye my hair?

34--Spelling Commonly Confused Words

Correct misspelled words in the following sentences. Example:

The Wizard of Oz is a master of allusion.

a. I'm out of breath after jogging.

b. Cheese and milk are dairy products.

c. This is the quite before the storm.

d. Ann lead the marching band yesterday.

e. I dressed up as a witch for the costume party.

1. Where you in class on Tuesday?

2. Please take the wrench off the car seat.

3. Thank you for the birthday presence you gave me.

4. I wish to respectively disagree.

5. I prefer the later, rather than the former.

6. The fable's morale is clear.

7. The criminal doesn't seem to have a conscious.

8. Did you choose wisely?

9. This lever is a handy device.

10. Did your friend give you good advice?

34--Spelling

© 1995 Simon & Schuster

Correct misspelled words in the following sentences.   Example:

My two sister-in-laws live in San Francisco.

a.   Our university employs eight coaches for its football team.

b.   The alumni want to see a good team each year.

c.   This is the forth year in five that the team has had a winning season.

d.   There is, of course, no way to insure that the team will continue to win.

e.   Given this record, though, the coachs probably won't altar much for next year.

1.   Tornadoes occur relatively frequently on the Great Planes in late spring and in summer.

2.   They are often accompanied by rain, hail, and lightening.

3.   Tornadoes themselves affect relatively small areas; there normally ten yards to a mile wide.

4.   The territory touched by a tornado is often razed.

5.   People have seen tornadoes move army tanks, farm combines, and railroad cars.

6.   As in the movie *The Wizard of Oz,* in which a tornado picks up Dorothy's house, tornadoes have moved whole houses.

7.   A tornado is able to brake nearly anything in its path, since its winds reach 300 mph.

8.   Most buildings are not tornado-proof, sense tornadoes carry such incredible energy.

9.   During a few minutes, a thunderstorm that produces a tornado might let lose the same energy as a one-megaton atomic bomb.

10. When human structures and tornadoes meat, the tornadoes normally win.

Review--Mechanics

Revise the following sentences if necessary. Example:

Five hundred
~~500~~-pound canaries say, "Here kitty, here kitty."

a. When he is a little hoarse, a speaker is like a pony.

b. The bare walked all day and moved only four feet because that was all it had.

c. My roommate thinks that having a well balanced meal is holding a slice of pizza in each hand.

d. When Little Red Riding Hood comments on her grandmother's big teeth, the wolf (who is disguised as the grandmother) replies, "The better to eat you with!"

e. Kent Conrad is a senator from North Dakota.

1. The *Monitor* and the *Merrimac* were the first two iron-covered ships to fight a sea battle.

2. Ground-Hog Day is on Feb. 2 each year.

3. Ralph Waldo Emerson encouraged self-reliance.

4. This is the best fitting pair of shoes I have ever worn.

5. This pair cost only one half of what my other pair cost.

6. I rode down the road in your car.

7. He drove South on Elm Avenue.

8. My neighbor is anti-gun control.

9. The speed limit is twenty-five miles per hour.

10. We read *Death of a Salesman.*

ESL 1--Count and Noncount Nouns

Underline count nouns once and noncount nouns twice in the following sentences. Example:

<u>Oxygen</u> is a <u>gas.</u>

a.   Hot air rises.

b.   Hot air balloons rise.

c.   I packed my clothing in the suitcase.

d.   I packed my equipment in the bag.

e.   Do you speak Spanish?

1.   Do you live in a house?

2.   Did you listen to the radio?

3.   Biology is my major.

4.   My major is biology.

5.   I had fun.

6.   She bought gasoline.

7.   She bought six gallons of gasoline.

8.   Did you bring your luggage?

9.   I am attending classes to gain knowledge.

10. Do you own a bicycle?

ESL 1--Singulars and Plurals

Change the verbs in the following sentences from singular to plural or from plural to singular if necessary. Example:

Chess ~~are~~ a challenging game.

a. My friends are in the restaurant.

b. Ice are cold.

c. The rains are early this year.

d. My shoes is wet.

e. Gasoline are expensive in northern Alaska.

1. My friend is in the restaurant.

2. Chinese are a language spoken by two of my friends.

3. Egg is an ingredient in many baked goods.

4. Three eggs is called for in this recipe.

5. My clothing are in my suitcase.

6. Computer science are my major.

7. The snow is falling.

8. Radios are displayed on the middle shelf.

9. Aluminum is a metal.

10. The coffee is bitter.

ESL 1--Singulars and Plurals

Add or delete determiners in the following sentences if necessary.
Example:

There are ~~the~~ computer terminals in this room.

a. Does she live in big house on corner?

b. I live in apartment near here.

c. The tomatoes are tasty in a salad.

d. This rice tastes good.

e. He has a few sheets of paper.

1. The university has built new library.

2. Shall we go to your room?

3. Did you buy the another car?

4. Her book is new.

5. Our bicycles are parked on the sidewalk.

6. The apples are my favorite fruit.

7. She has curly hair.

8. Did we get lot of rain?

9. We saw first movie.

10. Students who succeed take pride in their schoolwork.

ESL 2--Articles

Add or delete articles in the following sentences if necessary. Example:

The teacher brought a͟ umbrella into͟ classroom.

a. It was a honor to receive an award.

b. The national bird for United States is bald eagle.

c. My grandfather served on the battleship the U.S.S. *Missouri*.

d. The cats are the animals that many people keep as pets.

e. The Kennedys have been an important family in US politics.

1. I sat on cold, metal chair.

2. Is it an good idea to buy the hammer?

3. Clouds are covering the sun.

4. The robins are migratory birds.

5. Desk in my office is made of oak.

6. I accidentally broke the desk top, so I called carpenter.

7. My father planted onions in his garden last week. We will eat the onions in a couple of months.

8. Sand covered the beach. Where I stood, the sand was dry.

9. The serenity is a good state of mind to achieve.

10. I would like to work for FBI.

ESL 3--Adjectives and Adverbs

Underline adjectives once and adverbs twice in the following sentences. Example:

The big dog ran rapidly.

a. I ate two eggs.

b. I drank orange juice first, and then I ate two eggs.

c. He drove his new car rapidly.

d. He is rather quiet.

e. She never eats eggs.

1. They ran yesterday.

2. They ran slowly.

3. They both wore red jackets.

4. I never saw the movie.

5. I bought the large boat.

6. Sometimes I wonder if I needed it.

7. I would cheerfully return it if I could do so.

8. I often think of returning it.

9. I rarely go fishing.

10. I don't have time.

ESL 3--Subjects and Verbs

Underline subjects once and verbs twice in the following sentences. Example:

Roberto ordered a soft drink.

a.   The visitors said good-bye.

b.   They stood for a long time in the doorway.

c.   They seemed sad about leaving.

d.   The longer they stayed, the sadder I became.

e.   I was tired, and I wanted them to leave.

1.   The members of the team were tired and happy.

2.   They had played hard, and they had won.

3.   Years of hard work had gone into their excellence.

4.   Frank and Susan ski well.

5.   Frank and Susan enjoy skiing.

6.   The dog chased the cat.

7.   My neighbor owns both of these animals.

8.   He normally keeps them apart.

9.   Unfortunately, he forgot to shut the door to the house.

10. The dog and the cat ran in the house and knocked over two lamps.

ESL 3--Word Order

Circle misplaced words in the following sentences, then draw arrows to show where these words should be placed. Example:

Should wear I my red (big) coat?

a.   When should leave we?

b.   Are my blue new slacks in the closet?

c.   Yesterday I bought the last three tickets for the concert.

d.   Never we've heard this band before.

e.   I'm very excited about attending the concert.

1.   How did you like the concert?

2.   Was the concert good?

3.   Was that concert good!

4.   Did he drive his red big new car to the concert?

5.   The first song that the band played was very loud and happy.

6.   After the concert, we stopped at the little new restaurant on Elm Street.

7.   I ate incredibly a big cheeseburger.

8.   I had eaten two sandwiches and a red big apple only four hours earlier.

9.   I occasionally eat too much.

10. She says that she never overeats.

ESL 4--Prepositions

Ether change incorrect prepositions in the following sentences, or circle misplaced prepositions in the sentences and then draw arrows to show where the prepositions should be placed. Example:

When we meet ~~at~~ *on* Saturday, I want to get along ~~my parents~~ (with)

a. We should meet our friends in a few minutes.

b. We'll meet our friends at the restaurant.

c. Before we order, we'll look a menu at.

d. We need to get the bus off.

e. Look out for vehicles when we run the street across.

1. I'll have a birthday on a couple of weeks.

2. I'll have a party at the evening in my birthday.

3. I'll have the party in my apartment.

4. My apartment is in the brick building in the corner of Oak Drive and Fifth Street.

5. I need to figure out which games we'll play at the party.

6. Will you help me call our friends up to find out if they will be able to attend?

7. I'll speak half of them with, and you can speak the other half of them with.

8. I expect none of them will turn our invitation down.

9. I've made a list so we won't leave out any of our friends.

10. Should we look renting a movie into for the party?

73

ESL 5--Identifying Gerunds and Infinitives

Underline gerunds once and infinitives twice in the following sentences. Examples:

We will go <u>fishing</u> tomorow.

Shall we go <u>to see</u> a movie?

a.   We like to play cards after lunch.

b.   We particularly enjoy playing bridge.

c.   Do you promise to play bridge sometime?

d.   We plan to play cards again on Friday.

e.   We will try to play for an hour.

1.   The goldfish seem to want more food.

2.   I understand feeding them if they seem hungry.

3.   Would you recommend feeding them more?

4.   The pet store manager suggested feeding them this amount.

5.   Maybe we can visit the manager and ask.

6.   I have trouble imagining eating only a few crumbs.

7.   Please let me take you to the dance.

8.   I would like to take you to the dance.

9.   I fail to understand this physics problem.

10. Do you suggest discussing it with the professor?

ESL 5--Gerunds and Infinitives

© 1995 Simon & Schuster

Change gerunds to infinitives or infinitives to gerunds in the following sentences if necessary. Example:

I enjoy ~~to~~ play ^ing^ basketball.

a   I finished to write the paper this morning.

b.   I enjoyed writing the paper.

c.   A student asked handing in her paper tomorrow.

d.   The teacher gave the student permission to hand in her paper tomorrow.

e.   The student intends finishing her next paper on time.

1.   The lost child began to cry and screaming.

2.   We tried wiping the tears and to talk to the child.

3.   Peter Pan liked flying and to tease Captain Hook.

4.   Peter Pan didn't want growing up.

5.   Let me take you to the movie about Peter Pan.

6.   Will you please help me figure out the bus connections to the theater?

7.   Do you recommend to take the 12-A bus to Third Avenue?

8.   I recall taking this bus recently.

9.   I promise buying the tickets early.

10. Should we plan leaving at 3:30?

ESL 6--Modal Auxiliary Verbs

Follow the directions in parentheses when revising the verb(s) in the following sentences. Example:

I shut the door. (present ability)
(can written above "shut")

a. I work in the kitchen. (present ability)

b. I work in the kitchen. (present negative ability)

c. I work in the kitchen. (future advisability)

d. I work in the kitchen. (present preference)

e. I work in the kitchen. (past habit)

1. I read the book. (future necessity)

2. I read the book. (past advisability)

3. I read the book. (present advisability)

4. I read the book. (good advice)

5. I read the book. (possibility)

6. I live in Nebraska. (past possibility)

7. I live in Nebraska. (present preference)

8. I live in Nebraska. (past preference)

9. I live in Nebraska. (past plan)

10. I live in Nebraska. (past habit)

Review--ESL

Revise the following sentences if necessary.   Example:

I should go to class ~~yesterday~~. _tomorrow_

a.   Paula drove her new red big car.

b.   Look the car at!

c.   Paula parks her car in an garage.

d.   I might buy a car next month.

e.   I have a little money saved for a down payment.

1.   One of the most important inventions of the twentieth century are television.

2.   It brings current events, cultural events, and entertainment into our homes.

3.   The television set in my room is old.

4.   I carefully moved it from the living room in my parents' house to my room.

5.   I watch this television to keep up the news with.

6.   I also enjoy watching sports.

7.   You should visit me on Sunday, so we can watch the football game together.

8.   I was rather watch football than baseball.

9.   We can make some rice for dinner.

10. Should we flavor the rice with curry?

Answers to Lettered Exercises

7--Conciseness

Possible answers:

a. I liked the movie.
b. The ambulance driver decided to ignore the red light.
c. The menu lists fifteen different sandwiches.
d. John, a good athlete, wants to play professional football.
e. The speaker introduced the bill into the House.

8--Coordination

Possible answers:

a. The French Revolution began in 1789; it ended the thousand-year rule of kings in France.
b. King Louis XVI assembled the French Parliament to deal with France's huge debt, so the common people's section of the parliament announced it was France's true legislature.
c. King Louis appeared to disagree with this announcement, and a crowd destroyed the royal prison.
d. A constitutional monarchy was established, so some people thought the king would be content.
e. King Louis and the queen, Marie Antoinette, tried to leave the country, but they were caught, convicted of treason, and executed on the guillotine.

8--Subordination

Possible answers:

a. After the French Revolution began in 1789, it ended the thousand-year rule of kings in France.
b. King Louis XVI assembled the French Parliament to deal with France's huge debt before the common people's section of the parliament announced it was France's true legislature.
c. When King Louis appeared to disagree with this announcement, a crowd destroyed the royal prison.
d. Because a constitutional monarchy was established, some people thought the king would be content.
e. After King Louis and the queen, Marie Antoinette, tried to leave the country, they were caught, convicted of treason, and executed on the guillotine.

8--Coordination and Subordination

Possible answers:

a. The house was large, old, and drafty.
b. Correct.
c. Correct.
d. Correct.
e. Correct.

9--Parallelism

Possible answers:

a. Archimedes was an ancient Greek scientist, mathematician and inventor.
b. According to legend, Archimedes is supposed to have said "Give me the place to stand, and a lever long enough, and I will move the earth," and to have shouted "Eureka!" when he stepped into his bath and realized that he could measure the volume of an object by determining the volume of the water it displaces when submerged.
c. Archimedes discovered the principle of buoyancy, he discovered formulas for calculating the area of various geometric figures, and he invented the Archimidean screw.
d. According to the principle of buoyancy, boats float or balloons rise because they weigh less than the water or air they displace.
e. Correct.

9--Sentence Length

Possible answers:

a. Edward Teller, who was born in Hungary in 1908, is an American physicist. He is often called the "Father of the Hydrogen Bomb."
b. The small dog barked.
c. The dog barked fiercely.
d. After he jumped and wagged his tail, the dog barked.
e. The dog that I had petted barked.

10--Word Meanings

Possible answers:

a. The gardener's skin was sunburned.
b. The basketball player is tall.
c. Her perfume has a wonderful scent.
d. I bought Carl's car.
e. The cheeseburger cost seven dollars.

11--Word Impact

Possible answers:

a. Correct.
b. I think I'll fail accounting.
c. My mother is generous.
d. The door wouldn't close because the carpenters had hung it incorrectly.
e. After attending the funeral, we went to the graveside ceremony in the cemetery.

12--Nonsexist Language

Possible answers:

a. Jocelyn Elders is a doctor.
b. The Constitution gives every American freedom of speech.
c. Correct.
d. Correct.
e. Mike cleaned, took care of the children, and cooked.

Review--Sentence & Word Options

Possible answers:

a. A stool pigeon sits a lot.
b. Correct.
c. When Ted crossed poison ivy with a four-leaf clover, he got a rash of good luck.
d. When Ted crossed a lion and a mouse, he got a mighty mouse.
e. The gray animal that stamps out jungle fires is named Smokey the Elephant.

13--Main and Auxiliary Verbs

Main   Auxiliary

a. Jimmy Carter **was** president from 1977 to 1981.
b. He **defeated** President Gerald Ford in the 1976 election.
c. President Ford <u>would have</u> **been** president again if President Carter <u>would</u> not <u>have</u> **won** the election.
d. President Carter **was** known for his informality.
e. Ronald Reagan **became** president in 1981.

13--Transitive and Intransitive Verbs

Transitive   Intransitive

a. Jane <u>talked</u> slowly today.
b. She <u>spoke</u> too rapidly when she **gave** her speech yesterday.
c. The professor <u>leaned</u> forward and <u>listened</u> yesterday.
d. I <u>am</u> happy that she <u>spoke</u> slowly.
e. When I **give** speeches, I <u>speak</u> slowly.

13--Regular and Irregular Verbs

a. Correct.
b. Correct.
c. The water in the pool was cold today.
d. I have grown stronger as a swimmer.
e. Correct.

13--Irregular Verbs

a. Have you swum in this pool?
b. Correct.
c. Please lay the books on your desk.
d. Correct.
e. Erwin wore a blue shirt yesterday.

13--Verb Tense

a. I will have walked.
b. I walked.
c. I had been walking.
d. I am walking.
e. I will be walking.

13--Verb Tense, Voice, and Mood

a. Joan of Arc was a French military leader in the fifteenth century who said that God spoke to her in voices.
b. Correct.
c. Correct.
d. I wish that time travel were possible, so I could meet her.
e. I would find it interesting to meet Joan of Arc.

14--Singular and Plural Subjects

Singular   Plural

a. Gargoyles were used on many buildings during the Middle Ages.
b. A **gargoyle** is a sculpture depicting a grotesque or fantastic creature.
c. Often used to carry rainwater clear of a wall, gargoyles were used frequently on Gothic buildings.
d. The **rainwater** was normally expelled through the projecting mouth of a gargoyle.
e. At times, gargoyles were used simply for ornamentation.

14--Subject-Verb Agreement

a. Correct.
b. Some of the buses are overheated.
c. Correct.
d. The worst part of riding a bus is the waiting.
e. Seventy-five cents is the current bus fare.

15--Identifying Pronouns

a. Give **it** to **me**.
b. Give the ball to **me**.
c. Would **anybody** like to help **me** eat the pizza?
d. **This** is Mike's jacket.
e. Please pass the salt.

15--Pronoun Antecedents

a. Gilbert and Sullivan collaborated on many operettas; Gilbert wrote the lyrics and dialogue, and Sullivan wrote the music.
b. I like to study biological trivia; biology is my major.
c. In Montana people say that the cold keeps the riffraff out.
d. Correct.
e. Correct.

15--Pronoun Case

a. John, Sarah, and I ate the pizza.
b. Correct.
c. Correct.
d. Correct.
e. The coach praised my friend and me for our hard work.

16--Adjectives

a. The old car is **rusty**.
b. I drove the **rusty old** car.
c. The car is **old** and **rusty**.
d. The car--**old, rusty, decrepit**--belongs to my grandfather.
e. It holds **many** memories for him.

16--Adverbs

a. The fireplace was **very** hot.
b. The high temperature for that day was twenty below zero.
c. We **regularly** fed the fireplace huge chunks of ash.
d. The wind rattled the windowpanes and swirled the snow.
e. The bare trees swayed.

16--Using Adjectives and Adverbs

a. Correct.
b. Correct.
c. We didn't have any way to quiet the dog.
d. Correct.
e. Correct.

17--Sentence Fragments

Possible answers:

a. Correct.
b. Correct.
c. The word *balkanization* derives from the name of the Balkan Peninsula, which was divided into several small nations in the early twentieth century.
d. Bacteria at times present in incorrectly canned or preserved foods cause botulism, a type of food poisoning which is often fatal if not treated properly.
e. Melanie, in the film *Gone With The Wind,* is played by Olivia de Havilland.

18--Comma Splices and Fused Sentences

Possible answers:

a. Correct.
b. A huge engine probably powers a 1995 car, but a 2005 car might be powered by a small engine that produces energy to run electric motors for independently powering each wheel.
c. Correct.
d. Correct.
e. Correct.

19--Shifts and Derailed Sentences

a. I enjoy reading my horoscope, but I really wonder if it's ever true.
b. Correct.
c. Standing inside the penalty area allows a soccer goalie to handle the ball.
d. Arthur Ashe was the first black to win the Wimbledon men's singles tennis title.
e. August, 1961, is an important month because the Berlin Wall was erected then.

20--Misplaced and Dangling Modifiers

a. Barking loudly, the shepherd's dog ran toward the sheep.
b. Anxious to go home, the shepherd signaled her dog to herd the sheep.
c. Correct.
d. The shepherd had just bought her dog from a neighboring rancher.
e. The dog diligently herded the sheep home.

Review--Correct Grammar

a. The big hill knew the little hill wasn't telling the truth because the little hill was only a bluff.
b. Correct.
c. He said, "What do you call a conceited woman?--Mimi."
d. Correct.
e. Correct.

21--Comma Use

a. Correct.
b. For myopic people, distant objects appear blurred.
c. Correct.
d. Correct.
e. Myopia, therefore, is a visual defect which ordinarily can be corrected.

22--Comma Misuse

a. Although Canada's area is 4,000,000 square miles, its population is under 30,000,000 people.
b. Canada produces large quantities of wheat and beef.
c. Correct.
d. Copper, gold, nickel, and zinc are some of the abundant minerals in Canada's reserves.
e. Correct.

21 and 22--Unnecessary Commas

a. Correct.
b. Correct.
c. Correct.
d. Correct.
e. We drove 1,200 miles on Friday.

23--Semicolon Use

a. Correct.
b. "For tomorrow," the professor in my Bible as Literature class said, "read Genesis 1:1-10, Psalm 23:1-6, and Job 1:1-10."
c. Correct.
d. Douglas won the race against Lincoln to be senator from Illinois in 1858; he lost the race against Lincoln for the presidency in 1860.
e. Correct.

24--Colon Use

a. Correct.
b. I woke up at 6:45 in the morning.
c. Correct.
d. During the 1980's, the United States failed to reduce the national debt, win the war against drugs, or win the war against cancer.
e. The chaplain read Mark 1:1.

23 and 24--Semicolon and Colon Use

a. Although Steven Spielberg established his reputation by making adventure films, he made *Schindler's List*, based on historic fact, in 1993.
b. These adventure films include *Raiders of the Lost Ark* (1981) and *E.T.* (1982).
c. Correct.
d. Correct.
e. Correct.

25 and 26--End Punctuation and Apostrophes

a. Mexico's area is 761,000 square miles.
b. Correct.
c. Mexico's capital, Mexico City, is its largest city.
d. Mexico City's population in 1992 was nearly nine million, while New York City's population in 1992 was about seven million.
e. Mexico City's larger than New York City.

27--Quotation Marks

a. Have you read Dr. King's "Letter from Birmingham Jail"?
b. In the introductory notes to her compact disc *Mas Canciones*, Linda Ronstadt writes, "Since I was a young child, I have loved and admired the traditional music of Mexico in all its wondrous diversity."
c. Many people confuse "lie" and "lay."
d. Correct.
e. Correct.

28--Other Punctuation Marks

a. Correct.
b. Some bacteria--those that live in the digestive tract and aid digestion, for example--are beneficial to humans.
c. Correct.
d. In her poem "Chahinkapa Zoo," Louise Erdrich writes about the frustration wild animals in zoos must feel; the poem begins, "It is spring. Even here / The bears emerge from poured caverns. / Already their cubs have been devoured / by the feather-footed lynx caged next door."
e. Correct.

Review--Punctuation

a. Correct.
b. Jimmy is the man who breaks into houses.
c. Correct.
d. Correct.
e. Correct.

29--Capitals

a. Anwar Sadat was president of Egypt from 1970 until 1981.
b. Correct.
c. Correct.
d. Correct.
e. Three of the main factors that caused the assassination include (1) inadequate security for Sadat, (2) anger over his agreements with Israel, and (3) Arab nationalism.

30--Italics

a. Correct.
b. We traveled in a Boeing 747.
c. Is this a *3* or an *8*?
d. Correct.
e. Correct.

31--Abbreviations

a. Correct.
b. Correct.
c. Dr. Jocelyn Elders, who served the United States as surgeon general in 1992-93, grew up the daughter of a sharecropper in Arkansas.
d. Desiderius Erasmus was a leader during the Reformation who advocated studying the literature of ancient Greece and Rome, increasing personal piety, and changing the Catholic Church.
e. Correct.

32--Numbers

a. Correct.
b. Correct
c. Uranium's melting point is 1,132 degrees C, and its boiling point is 3818 degrees C.
d. Correct
e. Correct.

33--Hyphens

a. Correct.
b. Correct.
c. Correct.
d. Correct.
e. The more expensive coat is the better looking coat.

34--Spelling Plurals

a. Correct.
b. He was at two beaches yesterday.
c. Correct.
d. Correct.
e. Carl is one of my brothers-in-law.

34--Adding Suffixes and Spelling *ie, ei* Words

a. Correct.
b. I believe I will have my hair cut.
c. Did you paint the ceiling?
d. Correct.
e. Correct.

34--Spelling Homonyms

a. The bride and groom walked down the aisle.
b. Correct.
c. We went to the state fair.
d. Correct.
e. It is better to recycle paper, rather than wasting it.

34--Spelling Commonly Confused Words

a. Correct.
b. Correct.
c. This is the quiet before the storm.
d. Ann led the marching band yesterday.
e. Correct.

34--Spelling

a. Correct.
b. Correct.
c. This is the fourth year in five that the team has had a winning season.
d. There is, of course, no way to ensure that the team will continue to win.
e. Given this record, though, the coaches probably won't alter much for next year.

Review--Mechanics

a. Correct.
b. The bear walked all day and moved only four feet because that was all it had.
c. My roommate thinks that having a well-balanced meal is holding a slice of pizza in each hand.
d. Correct.
e. Correct.

ESL 1--Count and Noncount Nouns

Count   Noncount

a. Hot <u>air</u> rises.
b. Hot air **balloons** rise.
c. I packed my <u>clothing</u> in the **suitcase**.
d. I packed my **equipment** in the <u>bag</u>.
e. Do you speak <u>Spanish</u>?

ESL 1--Singulars and Plurals

a. Correct.
b. Ice is cold.
c. Correct.
d. My shoes are wet.
e. Gasoline is expensive in northern Alaska.

ESL 1--Singulars and Plurals

a. Does she live in the big house on the corner?
b. I live in an apartment near here.
c. Tomatoes are tasty in a salad.
d. Correct.
e. Correct.

ESL 2--Articles

a. It was an honor to receive an award.
b. The national bird for the United States is the bald eagle.
c. Correct.
d. Cats are animals that many people keep as pets.
e. Correct.

ESL 3--Adjectives and Adverbs

Adjective   Adverb

a. I ate **two** eggs.
b. I drank orange juice first, and then I ate **two** eggs.
c. He drove his **new** car rapidly.
d. He is rather **quiet**.
e. She never eats eggs.

ESL 3--Subjects and Verbs

Subject   Verb

a. The **visitors** said good-bye.
b. **They** stood for a long time in the doorway.
c. **They** seemed sad about leaving.
d. The longer **they** stayed, the sadder **I** became.
e. **I** was tired, and **I** wanted them to leave.

ESL 3--Word Order

a. When should we leave?
b. Are my new blue slacks in the closet?
c. Correct.
d. We've never heard this band before.
e. Correct.

ESL 4--Prepositions

a. Correct.
b. Correct.
c. Before we order, we'll look at a menu.
d. We need to get off the bus.
e. Look out for vehicles when we run across the street.

ESL 5--Identifying Gerunds and Infinitives

Gerund   <ins>Infinitive</ins>

a. We like <ins>to play</ins> cards after lunch.
b. We particularly enjoy **playing** bridge.
c. Do you promise <ins>to play</ins> bridge sometime?
d. We plan <ins>to play</ins> cards again on Friday.
e. We will try <ins>to play</ins> for an hour.

ESL 5--Gerunds and Infinitives

a. I finished writing the paper this morning.
b. Correct.
c. A student asked to hand in her paper tomorrow.
d. Correct.
e. The student intends to finish her next paper on time.

ESL 6--Modal Auxiliary Verbs

a. I can work in the kitchen.
b. I can not work in the kitchen.
c. I (should, ought to) work in the kitchen.
d. I would rather work in the kitchen.
e. I (used to, would) work in the kitchen.

ESL Review

a. Paula drove her big new red car.
b. Look at the car!
c. Paula parks her car in a garage.
d. Correct.
e. Correct.